THE VICTO
AND EDWARDIANS
AT WORK

John Hannavy

SHIRE PUBLICATIONS

First published in Great Britain in 2009 by Shire Publications Ltd,
Midland House, West Way, Botley, Oxford OX2 0PH, United Kingdom.
443 Park Avenue South, New York, NY 10016, USA.

E-mail: shire@shirebooks.co.uk   .   www.shirebooks.co.uk

A CIP catalogue record for this book is available from the British Library.

Shire Library no. 549   .   ISBN-13: 978 0 7478 0719 3

John Hannavy has asserted his right under the Copyright, Designs and Patents Act, 1988,
to be identified as the author of this book.

Printed in China through Worldprint.

09 10 11 12 13   10 9 8 7 6 5 4 3 2 1

COVER IMAGE
Pit Girls, Junction Colliery, Platt Bridge, Wigan, from a card posted in 1905.
.

TITLE PAGE IMAGE
Girls packing herring at an unidentified port in the Shetland Islands in 1904. The huge scale of the industry
can be gauged by the stacks of newly manufactured barrels behind the lines of girls.

CONTENTS PAGE IMAGE
'Wiltshire Bacon. The Ancient Custom – Burning the Pig' was one of a series of postcards on Wiltshire
customs and lifestyle published in the early twentieth century as part of the 'Famous Series' by Tompkins &
Barret of Swindon.

The author's own website can be found at www.johnhannavy.co.uk

Shire Publications is supporting the Woodland Trust, the UK's leading woodland conservation charity, by funding the dedication of trees.

CONTENTS

PREFACE

The idea of compiling a book about the Victorians and Edwardians at work has been with me for several years, and it is especially pleasing to see it come to fruition. With its companion volume *The Victorians and Edwardians at Play*, it commemorates a period when first the photographic print, and later the picture postcard, were the media through which British life was defined and celebrated.

As with every book I have produced over the past thirty-five years, although it is my name on the cover, the project is not the work of the author alone. It depends for its interest on the knowledge and input of many local historians and collectors who can add context and colour to the story each of these images has to tell us. My own collection of Victorian and Edwardian images – built up over more than thirty years of searching auction houses, flea markets, antique shops and junk shops – is the source of the majority of the pictures. I owe a growing debt of gratitude to the friends and dealers who continue to bring exceptional images and collections of pictures to my notice, and to the many people who have answered my questions about the images on these pages. The images from my own archive are augmented by a small number from the collections of the late Ben Norman, David and Marilyn Parkinson, Ron Callender, and the Ashbee-Gray-Lambert Collection. I am grateful for their generosity, and my thanks go also to Michael Gray and Alistair Gillies for their help and support.

Colour is the great thing in so many of these pictures – we are so used to seeing the past through monochrome or sepia photographs that to experience the Victorian and Edwardian world brought to life in these remarkable tinted images seems somehow to bring us a little closer to that world.

John Hannavy, Great Cheverell, 2008

In this picture, children are being trained in the Bolton cotton mills of John Kershaw & Sons. The employment of children as young as twelve was commonplace until outlawed in 1918.

William Henry Fox Talbot: 'Woodmen, Lacock', from a calotype negative probably exposed in the summer of 1845. The subjects were carefully posed to enable them to keep perfectly still for the long exposure, yet still retaining a sense of animated activity.

INTRODUCTION

Taking photographs of people at work is an application of the medium that is almost as old as photography itself. The first practical photographic processes date from the late 1830s and the very early 1840s. Both the French daguerreotype and the British calotype process came to public notice around that time, and the inventors and promoters of both were keen to demonstrate their versatility and usefulness.

The daguerreotype process produced a direct unique positive image on a small, silvered copper plate, highly detailed and as unique as a miniature painting, while the calotype produced a paper negative from which countless prints could be made. It was the calotype that proved to be the system from which photography would develop, but in the early days the promoters of both methods were keen to demonstrate the versatility of their respective processes.

Thus it was, probably in 1845, that the inventor of the calotype paper negative process, William Henry Fox Talbot, created the first planned 'occupational' photographs when he turned his crude wooden camera towards the 'woodmen' who worked on his estates in Lacock, Wiltshire. Earlier, a shoe-black had been photographed inadvertently in a Paris street in the late 1830s – he and his customer being the only living beings to remain still throughout the long exposure – but Talbot's pictures of his 'woodcutters' were planned and carefully composed, the 'workmen' positioned to convey a sense of animated activity while adopting poses they could hold still for a long period of time. Only one thing undermines the importance of this picture as the first of a genre: the subjects were not woodcutters at all, but Talbot's assistant, Nicolaas Henneman, on the left, and his groom, Samuel Pullen, on the right. What Talbot initiated, others developed into one of the most important uses of photography – giving history a priceless visual record of the Victorians and Edwardians at work.

As exposure times shortened through the 1850s, 1860s and 1870s, photography's ability to capture the real activity of people at work improved immensely. The camera went to war

The Manchester Ship Canal at Eastham, c.1900, published as a postcard before 1904. The three locks at Eastham marked the meeting of the canal and the River Mersey. In this view, a steamer is just about to enter the largest lock on her way out of the canal, while a sailing vessel waits her turn. The canal had opened six years earlier, in 1894, and, with the extensive docks constructed in Salford, had brought great prosperity to Manchester. So successful were the docks that the half-mile-long 'No. 9' dock, built on the site of Manchester racecourse, opened in July 1905.

for the first time in the 1850s: Roger Fenton's pictures from the Crimean War in 1855 are icons of early photography, although many of his pictures were of carefully posed groups.

Great industrial projects were photographed – showing men at work constructing the great bridges, ships and railway locomotives that drove Britain's development throughout the nineteenth century.

The popular process throughout much of that period was the wet collodion glass-plate process – a cumbersome process, and anything but user-friendly, but one which yielded the highest-quality images photography had yet delivered. The need to prepare and coat the large glass plates just before they were exposed in the camera, and to develop them immediately afterwards, required the photographer to take a portable darkroom with him wherever he travelled. Some highly ingenious designs for portable darktents were patented and advertised widely in the photographic press.

Above, top: Roger Fenton's 'photographic van' on location in Wales. As the collodion process required the plate to be coated with light-sensitive chemicals just before use and processed immediately after exposure, a portable darkroom was essential. Fenton travelled extensively throughout Britain with the van in the 1850s.

Above: A young man poses in front of an early steam trawler in Grimsby docks.

This much-reproduced line illustration is based on a quarter-plate daguerreotype showing Mr Jabez Hogg timing the exposure for his portrait of Mr Johnson – the earliest depiction of a photographer at work. The original photograph is part of the collection of the National Media Museum in Bradford. The caged bird at the top of the picture may be the origin of the phrase 'Watch the birdie'.

Talbot's printing establishment at Reading, photographed in 1845 or 1846, with a variety of photographic activities underway: (from left to right) copying a painting, making a portrait photograph, printing from calotype negatives, and photographing a sculpture. The device at the right is believed to be an early aid to focusing the camera. Talbot himself is operating the portrait camera in the centre.

Large numbers of people were employed in bringing photography to the general public. In addition to the photographers themselves, there were their assistants who carried and manipulated the equipment in the studio, on location and in the darkroom or darktent. All printing was done in contact with large negatives in the early decades, employing many women in making the significant numbers of prints that were offered for sale. Photographers were usually reluctant to appear in front of the camera, but one or two notable exceptions have left us with informative images of how early photography was produced. One of the earliest of these images shows Henry Fox Talbot's printing establishment in Reading in the 1840s, where many of the earliest published photographic prints in the world were produced.

Photographs were sold in print shops throughout Britain, and in the days before they started to appear in the daily newspapers the acquisition of photography required a positive decision on the part of the buyer. Today we receive much of the photography we see in a passive manner – having made the decision to buy the newspaper, we accept whatever images the paper publishes. At least until the 1890s, the customer made the decisions about which images to buy or not to buy. It follows, therefore, that the Victorian images that have survived today are those that were valued by their original purchasers – they are images that fulfilled an information need then, as now.

The advent of the picture postcard at the beginning of the twentieth century created a massive demand for innovative photography. With many postal collections and deliveries each day, the postcard became the primary means of regular communication.

FROM
TESTER & Co.
120, BOLD STREET,
LIVERPOOL.

Belgrabia

SILENT SEWING MACHINE.

MACHINES FOR TAILORS,
SHOEMAKERS, &c.

Price vertical Cover —
unpolished £7.7.0
Polished £7.10.0
double moulded table 7.15.0
Silver plated Medium 8.8.0

FROM
TESTER & Co.
120, BOLD STREET,
LIVERPOOL.

Belgrabia

SILENT SEWING MACHINE.

MACHINES FOR TAILORS,
SHOEMAKERS, &c.

Price with Cover complete
Bronze £8.10.0
Silver plated £9.3.0

Top left: 'Dress – the Wearer, Dress – the Maker', a carte-de-visite from c.1865 highlighting the differences in lifestyle between those who made the dresses for the wealthy and those who wore them. Cards making social comments like this are an interesting aspect of the early market in collectable photographs.

The mid-nineteenth century was a period of mechanisation, with numerous mechanical aids coming on the market. The treadle sewing machine was a case in point, with numerous models available for sale. Tester & Company of Bold Street, Liverpool, marketed machines on behalf of several northern manufacturers, and they used carte-de-visite prints as sales aids. On the backs of the cards were Tester's own label and details of the prices for different specifications of each machine. The machines illustrated here were made by Bradbury & Company of Oldham, Lancashire. There is something a little anomalous in offering sewing machines as being strong enough for use by 'Tailors, Shoemakers, &c.', but offering them silver-plated.

A ninth-plate ambrotype portrait of a boy soldier, late 1850s. When the ambrotype was first made, the boy's face would have been tinted, but the pigment has either faded or lost its adhesion, leaving only his red collar, red cap and tunic braid, together with his gold buttons and badge.

Postcards with messages along the lines of 'See you later today' are not uncommon, and it is hardly surprising that the senders of postcards liked some variety in the pictures they posted to their friends.

For a few golden years before the First World War, the picture postcard reflected the society that created it. Subject matter was as wide-ranging as the imagination of the publishers, and just about every aspect of working life, social life, landscape and architecture was featured.

As will be seen in this book, military subjects featured heavily on picture postcards before the end of the reign of King Edward VII, as did work in the mines and mills, on the farm and in the hop fields.

Local publishers produced extensive series of cards of local interest, featuring local employers and local people. In Wigan, Lancashire, for example, there were well over one hundred different locally published postcards available in the period 1905–10. While a number of them were the expected views of the town and its environs, most of them celebrated Wiganers at work: cotton-mill workers posing proudly for the camera in front of their looms or spinning frames, pit brow lasses in front of the coal screens, and miners in front of their pitheads. Two local publishers, Smiths and Starrs, vied with each other to produce the widest range of cards, the most delicately coloured, and so on. Wigan was no exception, and similar-sized towns elsewhere in the country boasted just as many cards.

Many of the finest coloured Edwardian cards were printed in Saxony, long renowned for the quality of its colour printing. Throughout the first sixty years of photography, all colouring was introduced by the artist's brush, but genuine colour photography was invented early in the twentieth century. However, when the French Lumière brothers introduced their autochrome process, it returned photography to a period of low sensitivity and long exposures. Real colour photographs – especially of animated subjects – remained highly unusual until well after the period covered by this book. As will be seen in the following pages, the artistry of the colourists was such that it is hard to tell which colour is genuine and which is artificial. Manuals started to appear as early as the 1850s, giving instructions on how to introduce natural-looking colour into the tiny cased portraits that were produced in their many thousands at that time.

For colouring daguerreotypes and ambrotypes, colourists often used dry powder pigments. The daguerreotype was often lightly coated with a gum to improve adhesion, but the collodion positive ambrotype image could be rendered tacky simply by breathing on it. With the passage of time, however, this has proved not to have achieved a strong enough bond, and the gentle blush tinting of cheeks has often lost its adhesion, leaving monochrome faces surrounded by coloured bonnets. Gilding was introduced either with powdered gold in a carrier, or by the application of gold leaf, and a 'jewel' effect was achieved with daguerreotypes by pricking the image to reveal the silver of the plate itself. For paper prints, colourists used water-based dyes that penetrated the paper surface itself, giving a permanent and effective coloured appearance. With the albumen print already having a cream base, the colourists had little to do to introduce realistic-looking skin colours. A very light wash with a weak red dye was all that was needed. For mass-produced coloured images like the coloured steroscopic cards that were popular throughout the 1860s, several colourists would be involved, each responsible for the application of a single colour or group of colours. Speed and accuracy were essential if costs were to be contained.

Photochrome prints, introduced in the 1890s, used multiple lithographic printings to add colour to black and white images – up to fourteen separate printings being used for some of the more realistic prints. With the advent of the coloured photographic postcard, a similar approach was used, although many fewer printings were employed; usually no more than four or five colours, and sometimes as few as three, if used with care, could create a realistic effect.

Many of the pictures in this book are, of course, from Edwardian postcards, and it is interesting to note just how early in the life of the photographic postcard the craze for card collecting started. Messages on the backs of cards as early as 1903 suggest that, while the postcard fulfilled a vital communication role, the collectability of the picture had a lot to do with the purchaser's choice. By the middle of the first decade of the twentieth century, collecting was recognised as a worldwide hobby, and the messages on the back of many cards – 'Another one for your album' and the like – testify to the hobby's popularity. That also meant that, like stamps, many cards were never posted. Indeed, some card designs were so popular as collectors' items in their day that finding one that has actually been used for the purpose for which it was intended gives today's collectors something of a 'buzz'.

Postcard collecting probably started in the United States; certainly the first magazine for collectors, entitled *The Postcard*, appeared in America as early as 1889. The magazine, however, was not enthusiastic about the proliferation of picture postcards, noting, with some regret, in an editorial in January 1894, that 'It is open to anyone to make such things and try and induce little boys to purchase them. We trust … that our readers will set their faces against such rubbish, or we shall be inundated with it. If we are to have special cards to remind us of every event that occurs in the history of a people, it is impossible to say where we shall be landed.' Little did they know just how popular the picture postcard would become, and how important it would be in offering us a window on the past.

By the early twentieth century some postcard publishers were printing 50,000 cards each day, and in 1903 it is estimated that the 37 million British people posted over 600 million of them – an average of about sixteen cards for every man, woman and child in the country! By 1910, the figures had increased by over 50 per cent. By the outbreak of the First World War, sending postcards printed in Germany was considered by some to be unpatriotic, but British colour printing was by that time catching up rapidly. Throughout the war years, and for many years afterwards (and thus outside the scope of this book), postcard publishers proudly proclaimed 'British manufacture throughout'.

That some of the postcard images in this book have been treasured for a century is a testament to the pleasure they gave those who received them. They form a unique part of our visual history.

Photographers were on hand to record the risks associated with working or travelling on the Edwardian railways. Here, workmen and railway officials are inspecting the wreckage after the boat train from Plymouth crashed at Salisbury station in the early hours of 1 July 1906.

The actress Nora Kerrin as Juliet: a tinted photograph by Studio Bassano, published as a postcard in 1908 by the Aristophot Company of London.

In this group of thespians who assembled for the first night of Sir Arthur Sullivan's play *Cox and Box* at London's Adelphi Theatre on 11 May 1867 were Quintin Twiss (who played Cox) and George du Maurier (Box). Also in the picture are Ellen and Kate Terry, who were appearing not in *Cox and Box* but in a play entitled *A Sheep in Wolf's Clothing* on the same bill. At this time Sullivan (front row left) had yet to team up with W. S. Gilbert, with whom his name would become forever associated.

ACTORS

In the days before cinema and television, theatres and music halls were the popular entertainment for the masses – everything from bawdy revues to the classics were staged up and down the country and, as a result, the theatre employed a great many people. Several early photographic studios made their reputation out of fine theatrical portraits.

The actors and actresses who trod the Victorian and Edwardian stage were often, like their counterparts today, 'resting'. There was other work available for them, and in the 1860s and 1870s actors and actresses willing to pose for staged theatrical tableaux, which were created and sold as stereoscopic '3D' photographs, were much in demand.

Companies such as the London Stereoscopic & Photographic Company produced many series of what are now known as 'genre' stereocards, some of them comic, others recreating moments from history, and many offering sentimental and romantic messages to their viewers. Just about every Victorian drawing room had a stereoscope for viewing these three-dimensional entertainments, and demand was kept high by competition between the major publishers, and the regular issuing of new sets.

Large numbers of people were employed in posing for the pictures, taking the photographs, printing them and colouring them by hand – a hugely labour-intensive operation which depended upon cheap labour to keep prices low. The prints, as well as being individually coloured, had to be cut out by hand and pasted on to the backing cards. Brown cards like the examples illustrated above and overleaf are relatively early – late 1850s and early 1860s. Later productions were sold on yellow cards.

Above: From the catalogue of the London Stereoscopic and Photographic Company, this card is entitled 'Crinoline Difficulties'.

Overleaf: An assortment of coloured genre stereoscopic cards from the 1860s, with groups of actors performing a variety of roles. From the top, they are 'The Bride', 'The Young Philosopher', 'The Murder of Thomas à Becket' and 'Evening Prayers'.

In 1905–6 Manchester photographer Percy Guttenberg was commissioned to take a series of photographs to be marketed as postcards by the city's Queen's Theatre, celebrating the stars who performed there.

These cards, posted to an address in Cork in February 1907, show (clockwise from top left) Miss Darragh and Mr Jerrold Robertshaw in *Antony and Cleopatra*, Mr Eric Blind and Miss Nora Lancaster in *Cymbeline*, Miss Ella Thornton, Miss Darragh and Miss Phyllis Relph in *Antony and Cleopatra*, and Miss Margaret Halstan in *Othello*.

IN THE ARMY

Left: Members of the staff of Lieutenant-General Sir George Brown pose for Roger Fenton's camera near Balaclava during the Crimean War, 1855. Many of Fenton's 360 photographs from the war were beautifully posed groups of officers and men. The long exposures necessary in 1855 meant that photography's ability to make casually observed 'snapshots' was still many years in the future.

Below: Bulford Camp, Salisbury Plain, 1905, with a cavalry regiment under canvas, the horses lined up neatly outside the tents. The publisher F. G. O. Stuart marketed an extensive series of military cards in the early years of the twentieth century.

Photography was only a few years old when the camera was first turned towards military subjects. From then on, military portraits were commissioned by the officers and men themselves as mementoes for their wives or loved ones, and by regiments to preserve the likenesses of their leaders and their heroes.

The camera first captured images of an army on the move in 1846, when American troops entered Casa Real in Mexico, and later photographs were produced of officers, men and equipment in just about every skirmish and war that took place.

The first commission to produce a series of images in wartime was given to Rochdale-born Roger Fenton by the Manchester publisher Thomas Agnew, to photograph the British forces in the Crimea in 1855. Fenton's images guaranteed his place in the history books, but they were taken 'at war' rather than 'of war'.

The camera was not yet capable of capturing action, so his images were either posed group portraits or scenes of camp life, together with a few images of the sites of battles – but not the battles themselves. Only in one image – 'The Valley of the Shadow of Death', strewn with cannonballs after a ferocious battle – does the horror of war come across. It would be decades later – in the Boer War – that photography was first able to capture the immediacy of battle.

Above: A fine studio portrait of a regimental sergeant-major in the 17th Lancers, c. 1855. As was often the case with these early 'ambrotype' or 'collodion positive' portraits, the image has been laterally reversed.

Left: A delicately hand-coloured ambrotype portrait of a bugler in full dress uniform, c. 1860. It can be assumed that this young man was born into a relatively wealthy family, as tinted ambrotype portraits like this were not cheap. It is housed in a thermoplastic 'union case' – the world's first use of moulded plastic – considered to be the height of Victorian sophistication.

Roger Fenton's study of 'Colonel Shadforth and the Officers of the 57th Regiment', from his 1855 Crimean War series, is an accomplished group portrait but, like every other military picture of the period, told very little about the war itself. By 18 June 1855 many of the men pictured here were dead – including Lieutenant-Colonel Shadforth himself, shot while leading his four hundred men in an assault on the Redan Fort near Sevastopol.

Above: This superb card by Valentine & Sons was posted in Aldershot on 5 November 1907 and bears the postmark of the 'Stanhope Lines'. It shows soldiers in full dress uniform returning to barracks after a church parade at St George's Church in Queen's Avenue, Aldershot. The sender was a newly appointed army chaplain from Rawtenstall in Lancashire, who wrote: 'This is the church to which I am attached. My Brigade is the 5th Infantry Brigade, and I am Chaplain to Gordon Highlanders, Royal Irish Rifles, and R.A.M.C. It is beautiful work and I have already made friends with my band boys.'

Right: The colour of the card on to which it is mounted suggests that H. B. Collis of St George's, Canterbury, took this military portrait some time between 1875 and 1881. The subject is a young officer in an unidentified regiment of foot. 1881 was a crucial date for uniform design, for it was in that year that the familiar shoulder straps were added, bearing the gilt metal rank badges.

H.B.COLLIS, PHOTOGRAPHER, ST GEORGES CANTERBURY.

The army played such an important part in so many people's lives that it is hardly surprising that photographers found a lucrative market in making 'likenesses' of soldiers and their loved ones. Professional photographic studios were established near most major barracks from the early 1860s, producing carte-de-visite size portraits.

BAKERS

Below: The workforce leaving Huntley & Palmer's factory in Reading, c.1907. The *Illustrated London News* noted twenty-five years earlier in 1882 that 'Huntley and Palmer's Reading biscuits have been in the mouths of most people. Three thousand pairs of hands are employed daily in their manufacture, yet, strange to say, nearly all the work is done by machinery. It is estimated that two thousand sacks of flour find their way into Messrs. Huntley and Palmer's factory weekly; and, when we remember how little flour is used in the manufacture of home-made pastry, some proportionate idea can be formed of the tons of butter, sugar, plums, currants, citron, ginger, and other ingredients that are used; but the number of cows and hens that must be employed by the establishment to produce new milk and new laid eggs is beyond our calculation.'

Bottom: Bakery workers cleaning their tins after taking bread out of the ovens in 1905.

THE VILLAGE BLACKSMITH

With a working horse needing a new set of shoes on average every six weeks, the blacksmith in a farming community had never been short of work. His livelihood was augmented by small light-engineering work and repairs to farm tools, his forge, hammer and anvil being used to turn out everything from a new set of shoes for a horse to a new blade for a scythe or a replacement coupling for a plough.

At the dawn of the picture postcard era, the horse was still the most widely used source of motive power – and not just on the farm. The growth of commercial traffic from factories and mills had brought about a significant increase in the use of heavy horses at the beginning of the twentieth century. There were many more blacksmiths employed in the industrial forges attached to engineering companies, coal mines and breweries than there were in traditional village smithies. Indeed, there were more horses employed in industrial locations than were at work on the farms, and they needed a substantial workforce of stablemen, grooms and blacksmiths to take care of them. Such artisans, however, lacked the romantic appeal of the village blacksmith and, while several of them were photographed at their work, very few were featured on postcards.

Opposite: Like the farming scenes later in this book, the idea of the blacksmith practising a centuries-old traditional craft was part of the idyll of the Edwardian countryside. The scene was ideal picture postcard material. Decades later, the same scene would grace jigsaw puzzles and the tops of chocolate boxes. 'The Old Smithy' was published c.1908, and within a very few years the horse's supremacy as the main source of power on the farm would go into decline. Stationary steam ploughing engines had been in use since the 1860s, and Garrett steam tractors had already started to appear on larger British farms.

Below: This postcard, 'The Village Smithy', comes from the 'English Farm Life' series which was published by Nottingham-based Boots Cash Chemists. The card, which dates from c.1904, was printed in Bavaria. At the time the Germans were considered to be much finer colour printers, although by the time of the First World War British printers had more than caught up with them. German cards were often produced without using the half-tone 'dot' screen, giving them a much more detailed quality.

BREWING

Barrels and brewery workers in the yard of the Haigh Brewery, Lancashire, 1890s. At that time every small town had at least one brewery producing ales to suit local tastes.

Drying hops in an oast house, an essential first stage in the beer-making process. This oast house was somewhere in Kent. The postcard was posted in Maidstone in 1905.

THE BUILDING TRADE

This sixth-plate ambrotype shows a group of brickmakers or tilemakers at work in the late 1850s, at an unknown location. The boy on the right is holding one of the brick moulds, while another mould is in place in front of the bearded man, waiting to be filled with the raw material being delivered by wheelbarrow.

With a huge expansion of building work throughout the nineteenth century, it is surprising that images of builders at work remain very scarce. This was a period of massive urban regeneration, with huge housing developments being constructed for the workers who flocked to the industrial towns. Photographers more frequently turned their cameras towards the prestige building projects than towards the humbler house-builder.

The photography of important buildings under construction can be traced back to the 1840s, when the construction of the Scott Monument on Edinburgh's Princes Street was photographed both by the pioneer calotypist Henry Fox Talbot and by the great Scottish masters of Talbot's process, David Octavius Hill and Robert Adamson. Despite the popularity of photography in the nineteenth century, and the subsequent huge market for unusual picture postcards in the Edwardian era, images of building and construction workers remain relatively uncommon.

BUS SERVICES

The first double-decker omnibuses in London – horse-drawn of course – were introduced as early as 1855. The 'upper deck' was no more than a few seats on the roof. If you travelled by bus in those days, you were expected to abide by a long list of rules, which included:

'Do not spit on the straw. You are not in a hog sty, but in a bus travelling in a country which boasts of its refinement.'

'Behave respectfully to females and put not an unprotected lass to the blush, because she cannot escape from your brutality.'

'Do not impose on the conductor the necessity of finding you change; he is not a banker.'

One of the London & Disctrict Motor Bus Company's double-deckers, introduced from c. 1907.

Most Edwardian bus companies produced and sold postcards of their fleets. This superbly coloured view, c.1903, shows a London General Omnibus Company's horse-drawn bus at Broad Street station in the City of London.

Motor buses first appeared in London in 1904, and the first motor double-deckers appeared within two years. By the outbreak of the First World War there were over three hundred. This postcard shows a 1907 double-decker from the London General Omnibus Company.

The three-man crew poses with what is clearly a brand-new double-decker just entering service with the London Motor Omnibus Company, c.1906.

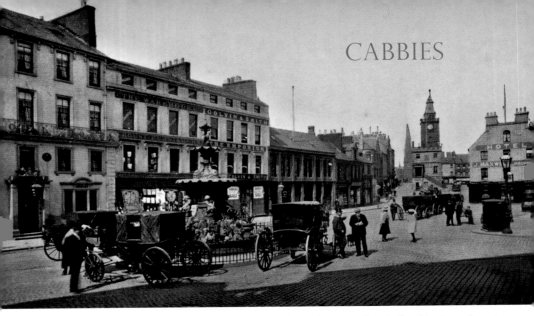

In Edwardian times taxicabs in most towns were still horse-drawn – as here in Dumfries in south-west Scotland. This photograph was taken c.1905 and remained on sale until well into the First World War, suggesting that the new-fangled motorised cabs had not yet reached the town.

Motor taxis were introduced into major cities in the early twentieth century and, as the decade progressed, they were introduced into larger towns as well. Photographs of these early cabs remain relatively scarce. The cab below, making its way through a flooded Paris street in 1909 with a horse-drawn charabanc following, is, like all early French cars, right-hand drive.

Tiger was one of a fleet of horse-drawn boats owned and operated by the Leeds & Liverpool Canal Company. These boats carried a wide assortment of cargo and worked the full length of the canal. This photograph was probably taken somewhere near Leeds and dates from 1908–10. Although at that time horse power was being replaced by steam barges, fast horse-drawn 'flyboats' were still in widespread use on the canal. New steam-powered flyboats, however, were already cutting journey times by more than half. The traditionally built wooden boats were also being replaced by iron-hulled craft. The cramped living quarters were at the rear of the boat and often housed whole families – parents and children.

LIFE ON CANALS AND RIVERS

Working the canals was never just a job – it was always a way of life. Entire families lived and worked on the narrowboats which plied the length and breadth of Britain through the network of canals which made up the waterways system. They provided a cheap and efficient – if not fast – cargo service, which survived for more than a century.

Their lifestyle can never have been easy; getting a fully laden barge through several locks a day was a slow and physically demanding task, and the families living in the cramped conditions on the boats cannot have enjoyed much privacy.

Wives and daughters decorated both their boats and their everyday utensils with brightly coloured motifs – many of them floral – to bring some much-needed colour to their lives. In so doing, they introduced an art form which endures to this day: even the static houseboats which today line many of our canals continue that tradition.

Eventually the greater efficiency of the railway caused the demise of much of the canal traffic, although coal and other heavy goods continued to be moved on the waterways until the closing years of the twentieth century.

In the twenty-first century canals are largely limited to pleasure traffic, but, as fuel prices and environmental concerns continue to rise, that may be about to change.

A barge, heavily laden with hay, makes its way along the River Thames past St Paul's Cathedral, c.1907. The Thames was the busiest and most polluted waterway in Britain, with large numbers of river craft travelling up and down the river from London's many docks.

A stately procession of sailing craft makes its way slowly through a lock at the northern end of the Caledonian Canal at Tomnahurich near Inverness in 1906. The canal offered a route diagonally across Scotland from Fort William to Inverness, cutting out the need to sail around the north coast and through the treacherous waters off Cape Wrath. Like many canals, its traffic today is predominantly pleasure craft.

Entitled 'Good News or Bad?', this fine study was taken by the Reverend William Wickham in 1891 and shows the 'boat examiner' delivering his report to a narrowboat family, probably in London. In the 1890s there was some concern about the worthiness of the craft that plied the canals – not unreasonably, considering the number of people who lived on board. The narrowboats in this photograph were operated by Fellows, Morton & Clayton.

A classic view on the Ellesmere & Chester Canal, photographed about 1905. Despite the smoking chimney on the barge, it is being hauled through the cut by a horse, which can just be seen in the middle distance on the towpath, towards the bridge. The smoke comes from the cooking stove.

THE CLERGY

Photography came along in the days before illustrated newspapers and when magazines were illustrated, but only sparingly, with expensive-to-produce woodblocks and engravings. So an early use for photography – especially after the introduction of the cheap carte-de-visite print – was the dissemination of pictures of the rich, the famous and the movers and shapers of Victorian society. By the early 1860s carte-de-visite prints of the leading members of the clergy were almost as popular as images of the Queen and her family, leading politicians, artists and entertainers. Such images found their way into hundreds, if not thousands, of Victorian family albums.

Above: An unidentified clergyman reads from a book, his Bible perhaps, in this early 1850s ninth-plate daguerreotype portrait by London photographer J. J. E. Mayall. Mayall was one of the most respected photographers of his day.

Right: Cardinal Nicholas Wiseman became the first Cardinal Archbishop of Westminster and head of the Roman Catholic Church in England in 1850, a time when it was being freed from many of the legal restrictions that had been placed on it since the Reformation. Having endured poor health for many years, the Cardinal died in 1865 and this portrait of him was taken only a few months before his death by the photographic studio Moira & Haigh. Portrait cartes-de-visite were also available featuring the Pope, the Archbishop of Canterbury and many other leading members of the clergy of various religions.

COOPERS

Coopers were much in demand during Victorian and Edwardian times. Barrels were used for beer and whisky of course, but their major use was for preserving fish. Most of the huge catches of herring landed in British ports were salted and packed in barrels, both for domestic use

and for export. The barrels were made of spruce — much of it imported from Sweden — strapped together with metal sleeves top and bottom, and with ash bindings in the middle. A cooper could earn a considerable amount of money in the early twentieth century if he worked fast.

Left: Newly made barrels stacked on the quay in Stornoway, Isle of Lewis, 1904.

Below: Coopers at work making barrel ends in Great Yarmouth, c.1906.

From the series 'Lancashire's Great Industry', this postcard of a typical cotton-weaving shed was posted in Burnley in May 1909. In an industry which typically employed huge numbers of women, this shed is an all-male domain.

THE COTTON INDUSTRY

Lancashire's cotton industry has all but disappeared. The huge mills which once employed thousands of people in Rochdale, Ramsbottom, Wigan, Bolton, Preston, Burnley and a hundred other towns have all fallen silent. Many have been demolished, and others converted to new uses. In Edwardian times, the cobbled streets of northern mill towns echoed to the sound of thousands of clogs as the workers made their way to the mills each morning. Over half a million people were employed in Britain's cotton mills at the time these postcards were produced.

The wide currency of the postcard – and huge sales – meant that there was a constant demand for new subjects, and many mill owners agreed to admit photographers to chronicle their working methods. Several series of postcards depicting the intricacies of cotton manufacture were published between 1905 and the outbreak of the First World War.

Work in the mills was long and arduous. To minimise the frequency of the yarn snapping, the weaving sheds were constantly sprayed with a very fine water mist, and the damp air was also laden with fine particles of cotton dust caused by the weaving process. Because of the working conditions, tuberculosis was commonplace and, according to contemporary reports, many of the women who worked in the mills had a pale emaciated complexion.

The pit brow girls of the Lancashire coalfield would rather work outdoors in all weathers than work in the mills.

In Leo H. Grindon's 1882 book *Lancashire: Brief Historical and Descriptive Notes*, the author is almost lyrical in his account of the county's huge cotton mills and their machinery: 'In the rooms and sheds devoted to weaving', Grindon wrote, 'the rattle of the machinery forbids even conversation, except when the voice is adjusted to it. In the quieter parts, the girls show their contentedness, not unfrequently, by singing. "How often", says the living type of the true Lancashire poet, most genial of his race – Edwin Waugh – "how often have I heard some fine psalm-tune streaming in chorus from female voices, when passing cotton-mills at work, and mingling with the spoom of thousands of spindles." That the girls, in particular, are not unhappy is shown by their preference of the cotton-mill to domestic service. Their health is as good as that of any other class of operatives; and though they have to keep upon their feet, it is not so long a time as young women in city shops. Of course there is a shadowy side to life identified with the factory. The hands do not live in Elysium, any more than the agricultural labourer does in Arcadia. The masters, as everywhere else, are both good and bad; in the aggregate they are no worse than their fellows in other places, and to expect them to be better would be premature. The wages are as good as those earned by any other large class of English workpeople, and if the towns in which so many thousands abide are unlovely, the Lancashire cotton-operatives at all events know little or nothing of the vice and filth of metropolitan St Giles.'

Grindon offers us an over-romanticised account of life and work inside the cotton mills – had there really been any singing of psalms in the sheds, it would have been inaudible both

within the mill itself and outside, lost beneath the din of the looms and spindles. Lip-reading was the normal means of communication amongst the girls, and premature deafness was not uncommon.

These were days long before the understanding of 'health and safety', and decades before the introduction of ear protectors. The damp in the mills, with cotton dust flying everywhere, was also a significant health hazard. Working in the mills did, however, offer the girls their first taste of freedom: away for the first time from the dominant influence of their mothers, many mill girls developed friendships which endured for their entire lives.

Two mill girls pose for the camera outside Gidlow Mills, Wigan. The mill's wealthy owner, John Rylands, founded the Manchester University library named after him.

The publishers of the 'Lancashire's Great Industry' series of postcards, L. Pickles & Company of Bradford, would have been aware of the instructional value of their cards. Through these superbly produced cards, the many skills and procedures involved in cotton spinning and weaving were made familiar to a wide public who had never been near a cotton mill. Indeed, towards the end of the Edwardian era, the postcard format was used to create instructional reminders for the workforce about the need to work safely. Such cards were issued to workers who had been observed either misusing equipment or working in a manner likely to harm themselves or others.

The workforce of John Rylands' Pagefield Mill in Wigan was quite used to posing for photographs. Local publisher Will Smith marketed an extensive series of postcards of the cotton-manufacturing process in the early twentieth century. This was the card room.

As the mill was engaged in every aspect of the process from raw cotton to finished cloth, it was an obvious choice for photography, and the workforce seemed happy to co-operate.

CUTLERY MAKING

Metalworking in Sheffield goes back probably to the time of the Romans and has been one of the city's major industries for the past two centuries. While high-quality steel for a wide variety of industrial applications was always the mainstay of the industry, the name of Sheffield became synonymous with fine cutlery in the nineteenth century – so much so that the town's pre-eminence in its manufacture was celebrated in a series of beautifully photographed postcards in 1904/5.

While industrial steel-making was centred along the Don valley, cutlery manufacture – and the manufacture of high-quality steel instruments – developed on the hillsides to the south and west of the city. Silver plating was pioneered in Sheffield in the middle of the eighteenth century, and by the middle of the Victorian era Sheffield plate had become renowned the world over.

A few years after the end of the Edwardian era, in 1914, the process for making stainless steel was discovered in Sheffield, underlining the importance of the industry, and ensuring the continuation of the manufacture of high-quality steel throughout the twentieth century.

Above: 'Metal buffers' polishing forks and spoons, c.1904/5. Considerable numbers of women were employed in the finishing processes.

Opposite: Knife grinders in a Sheffield cutlery factory, c.1904. This card was sent to a young postcard collector in London in August 1905, and described as a 'real Sheffield card'.

Cross-Channel steamers being prepared by dock workers at Dover's Britannia Pier in the late 1890s. These coal-fired paddle steamers had much larger crews in their engine rooms than today's far bigger vessels – and today's cross-Channel ferries are monsters by comparison. Teams of stokers spent the entire journey shovelling coal to keep the boilers producing steam.

A group of workers watching ships entering the Canal Lock at Gravesend, from a postcard sent in 1906. The Gravesend & Rochester Canal linked the Thames with the Medway but was not a commercial success. The Gravesend canal basin is now being renovated and redeveloped, having been allowed to deteriorate since the canal closed in 1934.

Dockers unloading bales, perhaps of cotton, from a cargo steamer on to a waiting barge in the Pool of London, 1908. This postcard, 'chromotyped in Germany', was specially produced for sale in Selfridges.

DOCK AND HARBOUR WORKERS

Work in the many docks and harbours around Britain's coast was casual, gruelling and insecure. By long-established custom, the dockers waited at the dock gates in the hope of being 'called on' and offered a day's work. For the workers, it was an uncertain occupation, dependent entirely upon the arrival of ships to be worked on. With hundreds, if not thousands, of ships arriving in British ports most weeks, a huge workforce was needed, but much of the work was seasonal, bringing much hardship to the dockland communities. In slack summer periods in the London docks, for example, many workers went hop-picking with their families in Kent (see page 76).

There was, moreover, a strict hierarchy of labour, with archaic job titles such as 'coal-whippers', 'coal-backers', 'coal-porters', 'ballast-heavers' and 'lumpers', all seen as quite distinctive roles within the docks. In the days before extensive mechanisation, loading and unloading ships was an intensely physical activity. According to Henry Mayhew in *London Labour and the London Poor* (1861), coal-backers, for example, who worked in teams of five, earned less than a shilling a ton for 'carrying coals on our backs from ships to wagons'.

A successful, if protracted, strike in the London docks in 1899, over a demand for an end to contract work (payment per ton moved) and its replacement with a wage of sixpence (2.5p) an hour, is recognised as one of the pivotal demonstrations of the power and importance of the trade-union movement.

Entitled 'Farewell to Orkney', this unusual photograph depicts cattle being hoisted in cradles into the forward hold of a steamer at Stromness. The ship is the North of Scotland, Orkney & Shetland Shipping Company's ferry *St Ninian*, of 702 grt (gross registered tonnage), which served the route from 1895 until 1948. A regular steamer crossing between Scrabster on the Scottish mainland and Stromness was introduced as early as 1855 and continues to this day.

A great storm causing extensive damage brought the photographer James Date to Watchet harbour, Somerset, in July 1861. The result was a series of ambrotype views showing the repairs in progress. He had to have the total compliance of his subjects. The people in these views would have had to stand still for the long exposures while the pictures were made. Date operated his studio in Watchet at least until the early 1880s. The plate on which the positive image is carried was the actual plate exposed in the camera, so there was no negative from which further prints could be made. He advertised such views for sale, and so each image that he sold would have been slightly different from the others.

Crewmen prepare to cast off one of the ferries at the jetty in Portsmouth harbour in 1902. Behind them is the Royal Yacht *Victoria and Albert*, visiting the port while King Edward VII reviewed the 'Fleets of All Nations' as part of the Coronation Review at Spithead.

Cargo and provisions being loaded on to a liner at Liverpool Landing Stage in 1905. It is noteworthy that, despite the date, all the vehicles in the photograph are horse-drawn.

DOMESTIC
SERVICE

From a series of cards published for the benefit of those stationed in what the back of the card proclaims to be 'British India', c.1905, comes this fine study of a 'domestic servant'.

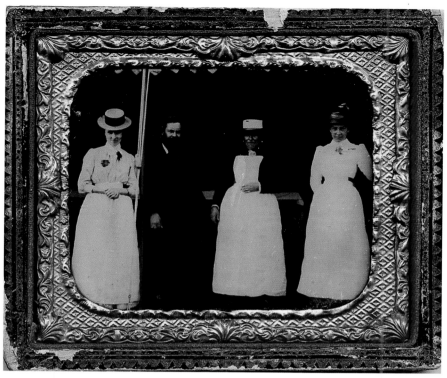

This early sixth-plate ambrotype unusually
shows a domestic servant posing for the
camera alongside three fashionably dressed
people – presumably her employers – at
the entrance to a grand marquee. In the
interior of the tent, tables can just be
discerned covered with white linen
tablecloths, being prepared for a meal.

The Pictorial Stationery Company produced
'character' postcards c. 1908, depicting local
people, costumes, customs and lifestyles.
A youth on his way to get some fresh milk
– or perhaps beer from a nearby inn –
stops to talk with a servant girl in a back
street in St Ives, Cornwall, creating a
somewhat unusual postcard subject.

'Busy Bees' is typical of a style of postcard which celebrated the dignity of domestic service and hard work. Hundreds of cards of this type were published in the years before the First World War. Like a large proportion of the tinted cards available at the time, this card was printed in Saxony.

'Did You Call, Sir?', from one of the London Stereoscopic Company's popular and interminable 1860s series of humorous cards, played to the music-hall image of the relationship between master and servant. Others showed such 'indiscretions' as the master being found in the kitchen with flour-covered handprints on the seat of his trousers!

On the assumption that anything French was a bit naughty, the scene on this staged 1860s stereocard revelled in the title 'L'Absence des Maîtres' and shows the servants having a great time living it up in the drawing room when their master and mistress were presumably safely out of the house!

Before the First World War radically changed the social order, having servants was not a privilege enjoyed exclusively by the upper class. Even a humble village schoolmaster would be expected to employ a maid and a housekeeper. Books on cookery and housekeeping invariably contained some advice on how the lady of the house should treat her domestic servants. Countless editions of Mrs Beeton's *Book of Household Management* lamented the fact that some mistresses 'do not, when engaging a servant, expressly tell her all the duties which she will be expected to perform. This is an act of omission severely to be reprimanded. Every portion of the work which the maid will have to do should be plainly stated by the mistress, and understood by the servant.' She also identified the loyalty of the servants as being something that the lady of the house needed to consider and observed that if her servants 'perceive that the mistress's conduct is regulated by high and correct principles, they will not fail to respect her'.

Above: This early 1860s sixth-plate ambrotype portrait of a nanny with her charge is unusual. Photography at that time was still very expensive, so was posing for this portrait her own idea, or suggested and paid for by her grateful employers?

Above left: The refectory at Stonyhurst College, the Jesuit public school in Lancashire, in 1858. Published in the *Stereoscopic Magazine*, this photograph shows the school's domestic servants preparing for the boys' main meal of the day.

Left: A servant girl hands out glasses of water at the Original Chalybeate Spring in Tunbridge Wells, 1907.

The Hill & Saunders studio in Oxford for decades had almost a monopoly of the photography of academics in the city. They photographed the dons and the graduates each year, offering superbly produced carte-de-visite portraits like this, presented in beautiful leather cases. The academic may not look particularly happy, but then academia in Victorian times was not considered to be a world for the frivolous. He may also have been rather uncomfortable at the time, his head held in place by a metal head-clamp during the long exposure. The clamp would have stood just behind his chair.

EDUCATION

It is not certain when the camera was first turned towards the world of education, but school photographs started to appear relatively early on – first of all catering for the more affluent end of the education system. It was not long, however, before that most ubiquitous of photographic media, the carte-de-visite print, started to reflect the school days of the poor as well as the privileged – class groups which included children with holes in their jumpers can be found as early as the beginning of the 1860s.

At the upper end of the social scale, studios such as Brachers in Oxford entered the market in the late 1840s, and Hill & Saunders started producing graduation pictures before 1860. This was an era when access to university was largely restricted to the upper and upper-middle classes, so the cost of having portraits made by exclusive studios was not a problem.

Especially in rural communities, the Victorian and Edwardian schoolmaster was an important and respected member of local society and thus had to be seen to maintain a lifestyle appropriate to his social status. Although teachers' salaries were never generous, he and his family were, for example, expected to employ a servant.

This carte-de-visite group photograph shows Class 6 from Weymouth House Boys' School in Bath in the early 1860s — apparently with two teachers for a group of twenty-two boys. The photographer is unknown.

The new Georgian era had only just replaced the Edwardian period when this picture was taken in 1910 and, with a portrait of the new king already framed and on the wall, children posed with their teacher for a delightful classroom photograph. Here, one teacher has a class of twenty-eight children.

ENGINEERING

Above: From an extensive series of postcards published c.1910, this view shows the interior of the steel foundry at the huge Vickers works at Barrow-in-Furness. Ironfounding, and later steel-making, had become one of the most important industries in the Furness area in the second half of the nineteenth century, largely because of the availability of locally mined haematite in the Barrow and Ulverston areas, and Barrow's industrial expansion in the late nineteenth century was driven by the iron and steel works. Leo H. Grindon, in his book *Lancashire: Brief Historical and Descriptive Notes* published in 1882, had observed that Barrow was fast becoming a centre for iron-smelting, and assured his readers that the future for this developing industry looked very good indeed. The availability of local steel led directly to the establishment of Vickers' huge shipyards, which at their peak covered over 100 acres. The Sheffield steel company Vickers had taken over the Barrow factories and shipyards in the closing years of the nineteenth century. Shipbuilding in Barrow – especially warships – continued throughout the twentieth century, and today Britain's nuclear-powered submarines are still built in the town.

Opposite: The location of this engineering shop, c.1890, is unknown and the scene is typical of hundreds of similar manufacturing sites across the country. The steam hammer was a standard feature of heavy machine shops like this and was used to fashion machine parts for shipping, mining, the railways and a thousand other applications. Rigby's patent steam hammers had been manufactured in Glasgow by Glen & Ross since the early 1860s. The importance of a ready supply of cheap labour is underlined by the realisation that the process of feeding the large metal casting into the steam hammer apparently required eleven men – and a boy watching from behind the machinery! To the right of the hammer, an elegantly dressed gentleman with top hat and cane, presumably the manager or owner, watches the proceedings.

EXHIBITIONS, ADVERTISING & PROMOTION

When Prince Albert, Queen Victoria's consort, began to promote the idea of holding a Great Exhibition in London in 1851 to celebrate the diversity of life, culture and industry across the Empire, few imagined that it would be the immense cultural and financial success that it was. Even fewer would have believed that it would be the start of an 'exhibition culture' that endures to this day, and would give birth to a range of support industries and professions. That first Great Exhibition attracted 14,000 exhibitors, and over 6 million visitors, generating a profit of almost £250,000.

Each successive exhibition employed more people, and each concentrated on reaching potential clients. The salesman, the marketing expert and the exhibition designer became increasingly evident.

The souvenir, gift and postcard stall at London's 1908 Franco-British Exhibition sold a wide range of mementoes of the event, including the actual postcard reproduced here. The exhibition ran from April until October and was constructed on a 140-acre site in the Shepherd's Bush area of London, which has ever since been known as 'White City' – a reminder of the white plaster finish of the exhibition buildings, many of which survived for decades after the exhibition closed. The site offered employment to thousands of people during the exhibition, and at the many other events which subsequently made use of the buildings. Parts of the site and the newly built stadium were also used for the 1908 Olympic Games, but while there are many cards of the exhibition site, postcards of the Olympics do not seem to have been produced in large numbers.

Ballymcclinton, 'a typical Irish village', was created and populated by the makers of McClinton's soap as an advertising promotion during the Franco-British Exhibition at the White City in 1908. The exhibition was still open to visitors in the following year. Postcards – and postmarks – described the location as the Shepherd's Bush Exhibition.

Above: From F. Hartmann's lengthy 'Rural Series' of views of daily life on the farm, this postcard is entitled 'How Blithely Do They Drive Their Teams Afield' and dates from around 1906. The design of the plough being used suggests that the photograph was taken in spring when a lighter ploughshare was commonplace – the heaviness of the soil having been loosened by the frosts and snows of winter. Several designs of plough from this period had wheels at the front to control the depth of the cut and make for more even ploughing, but without such aids the skill of the ploughman was paramount.

Opposite: This magnificent postcard of a farmer and his heavy horse, titled 'The Ploughman', was posted in Birkenhead on 21 March 1907. It was sent by 'Aunt Mary' to her nephew in nearby Rock Ferry and carried the message:'I could not resist sending this for your album. Is it worthy of a place? He's got such a Kent-like face, hasn't he?'

ON THE FARM

Farming at the beginning of the twentieth century was a way of life which had changed very little in hundreds of years. Hugely labour-intensive, it employed vast numbers of people on low wages and fed a nation which was still largely self-sufficient in fresh food.

The ploughman walking behind a pair of massive horses was a common sight, as it had been for centuries. His skills were passed on from generation to generation, and the accuracy and symmetry of his ploughing was a matter of immense pride.

As a romantic postcard subject, farming had very few peers, and its instructional value should not be overlooked either. For little-travelled city folk, postcards showing farming life, and the many and varied processes of food production, were highly informative.

From the 'Farm Life' series of views, this 1905 postcard is entitled 'Farm Life – Carting'. The dried sheaves of corn being loaded on to the cart by the four farm hands would probably have had only a very short journey. At the edge of the field, there would have been a mechanical threshing machine, driven by a long belt connected to a steam traction engine. Steam engines had been used in harvesting for about fifty years before this picture was taken.

This postcard, 'Making Hams and Bacon – A Hungry Family', was published in London in 1907, and was posted in Shrewsbury in January of the following year. No farming subject was too obscure for the postcard market, and one must presume that the farmer got some sort of payment for posing for the camera – perhaps a number of the cards? Such cards were of educational value as well as social, especially for those who never visited the countryside.

This view of harvesting with a horse-drawn reaper in the Sussex countryside was sent to a corporal in the 1st Troop, 'O' Squadron, 5th Dragoon Guards, stationed at the Curragh Camp in Ireland, by his sweetheart, Rosemary, in the summer of 1910. Pastoral images like this were hugely popular. Titled 'In Nature's Realm', it too idealised the English landscape and the lifestyle of the farmer. The reality was often very much harder.

Printed in Saxony, and published by Lowe, Willets & Company of Birmingham, 'The Reapers, Homeward Bound' comes from a long series of pictorial cards depicting life on the land, published in the early years of the twentieth century. It was posted in Kidderminster in January 1909. All these cards demonstrate a pride in labour – workers in every trade seem to have been happy to be photographed and for their images to be used in this way.

Top: With a small boy astride the horse, 'Loading Hay', a postcard from about 1906, underlines the fact that farming involved all the family – young and old alike.

Welsh Farmer's Daughters.
754·
[Copyright.]

Opposite page, bottom: 'Getting into Harness', showing a farmer about to start harrowing his field with his two magnificent horses, was published by Wildt & Kray in London in 1908, No. 1153 in their series of postcards.

Left: In the 1870s the London Stereoscopic Company produced many series of hand-tinted stereoscopic and carte-de-visite sized images to be bought and collected. This carte-de-visite, purporting to show a 'Welsh farmer's daughter', came from a lengthy series of studio portraits of customs, costumes and curiosities. It was No. 754 in the series, so there was little likelihood of the collector running out of cartes to purchase. These images were designed to fit into the family portrait album, and character cartes and scenic views were bought by holidaymakers, in the same way that postcards were collected throughout the twentieth century.

Below: 'A Halt by the Window': the day's work over, the horses are being fed some titbits by children as they pause by a cottage window.

Above: Photographed in 1909, this idyllic rural scene, 'Haymaking at Chilham Castle, Kent', was published by a Maidstone company.

Below: Beneath the great Westbury White Horse in Wiltshire, 1904, a farmer watches over his sheep.

Opposite: 'Shawin' Turnips', photographed c.1905, is perhaps the strangest farming card of them all but demonstrates some of the hard work the farming community had to cope with. Then, as now, turnips were a staple food for both people and animals during the winter and were kept under straw and earth throughout. Potatoes were stored in much the same way.

A London fire brigade rushes towards a fire in 1906. This card was posted in Ross-on-Wye, Herefordshire, in January 1907.

THE FIRE SERVICE

In the seventeenth century, fire fighting was carried out by small teams of firemen employed by insurance companies. The company insuring a particular building would affix a small plaque to the building when the premium had been paid. In the event of fire, firemen from several insurers might turn out – equipped with no more than small hand-drawn and hand-cranked pumps – and if it was a rival's plaque on the building, they might go away. Some stories, hopefully apocryphal, suggest some might even have stayed and watched the building burn!

The first formally established municipal fire service in Britain was in Edinburgh – set up in 1824 – and that was followed four years later by the establishment of the Manchester Fire Brigade.

London first got a single unified fire fighting service in 1833 – the London Fire Engine Establishment – as a direct consequence of a group of insurers recognising that it was actually in their best financial interests to organise a faster response to fires in the capital. At that time there were just over a dozen fire stations in the city, almost all still using hand-pumps.

Steam-powered fire engines first appeared in London in 1829, when Braithwaite and Ericsson, trialled a prototype engine for London. It didn't catch on – its thirst for water was greater than the water mains of the day could support! In any event, the first director of the new fire service was not very enthusiastic about the value of the steam-powered pumps. The great fire which destroyed the Houses of Parliament in 1834 might just have been brought under control more quickly if the increased capacity of the steam pumps had been available!

It was the 1860s before these engines started to enter general use – and of course they could pump a lot more water per minute than their hand-cranked predecessors. The London Metropolitan Fire Brigade was set up in 1865, and its new superintendent was an enthusiastic supporter of steam-powered equipment. He also considerably increased the number of fire stations in the city, improved the training of firemen, and established many of the principles of fire fighting which have been further developed over the past century and a half.

By Act of Parliament, the London Fire Brigade was formally set up in 1904, and by the time the postcard photograph on the left was taken, the brigade was experimenting with petrol-driven vehicles – the first having been trialed (unsuccessfully) as early as 1902. Horses, however, were found to be faster and more reliable than the motorised engines!

Amazingly, there were still many voluntary fire services up until the time of the First World War, and professionally trained and manned fire brigades were not required by law at that time. It would be 1938 before a law was passed requiring the establishment of local fire authorities – giving every citizen the right for the first time to have a fire at their premises tackled free of charge by professional fire officers.

Even into the twentieth century, private fire services were commonplace, taking responsibility for fire safety in large mills, factories, docks and harbours. This photograph, taken c.1910, shows the seventeen-man brigade maintained by a Lancashire cotton mill.

Glasgow's firemen were called into action just after midnight on the morning of 17 August 1909 when an enormous fire, apparently started by a gas explosion, broke out in a block of warehouses in Ingram Street. The explosion and fire demolished an 80-yard stretch of buildings on the north side of Ingram Street, between High Street and Shuttle Street. Such was the interest in the event that postcards were published by Valentines of Dundee within forty-eight hours of the fire. This card was posted on 21 August to Miss Galbraith in Herne Hill, London, by her nephew Jack, who had witnessed the fire and believed it was 'the biggest one that has ever been in Glasgow'. Certainly the fire took all night to bring under control, and the cost of the damage was estimated at £250,000, an enormous sum at the time.

FISHERMEN & FISHWIVES

This Cornish fishwife posed for a photograph some time before 1900, and her picture was first used on a postcard published by Raphael Tuck in 1901.

'Scotch Fisher Girls at Scarborough', from a postcard c.1906. The daily task of bringing the fish ashore, gutting and cleaning the catch and repairing the nets employed large numbers of men and women. On the back of the card, the sender, David, notes: 'This is a picture of the girls – there are hundreds of them here!' Unusually, the barrels seen here seem to have just one metal band rather than two, and two ash bindings.

Herring gutters and packers, Great Yarmouth, 1904. Like the Scarborough girls above, these were Scots girls who travelled each year to work in English east-coast fishing towns such as Scarborough, Great Yarmouth, Grimsby and Lowestoft. Each barrel they packed contained upwards of one thousand herring, and in 1905 they were paid 8d (3p) per barrel of fish gutted and packed.

The two great Scottish photographers of the 1840s, David Octavius Hill and Robert Adamson, were the first to photograph the fishwives of Newhaven on the Firth of Forth, and when the picture postcard started to appear in the early years of the twentieth century photographers returned to those same subjects for their inspiration.

In the years before the First World War, in fishing ports as far south as Lincolnshire, many of the women who gutted and cleaned the fish were Scottish – itinerant working women who went where the fish were. In some cases, photographs taken years earlier were tinted and reissued as postcards.

On the left of the picture, a group of fisher girls on the quayside at Arbroath in the early 1900s are packing herring, while, on the right, the local coopers are sealing the filled barrels.

The herring fleet setting sail from Peterhead harbour, c.1905. Despite the growing popularity of steam trawlers, many of the fishing ports in north-eastern Scotland still depended on sail.

'Off to the Fishing, Great Yarmouth'. Trawlers of the Great Yarmouth fleet are towed out of the harbour by one of the three paddle-steamer tugs operated by Nicholson Towage and based at the port. This one was the *Tom Perry*, built in 1879, which had been disposed of by 1909, placing this photograph sometime between 1901 and 1909. The other two tugs to work the port in Edwardian times were the *Gleaner* and the *Reaper*.

Landing herring at the fish wharf, Aberdeen, c.1905. It was once said that every trawler at sea created one hundred jobs ashore, making an estimated total workforce in 1905 of one million people.

GAMEKEEPERS

The gamekeepers on the great Victorian and Edwardian estates were key members of staff, for their management of the game and its protection from predators, were crucial in enabling the landowners to enjoy a full and varied diet. The keepers also played a pivotal part in the preparation for the 'sport', which began each year on the 'Glorious Twelfth of August'. They were highly skilled land and stock managers and well versed in the annual cycles of nature, able to nurture stocks of fish, deer, game and fowl, and to control the pests and vermin that might undermine their efforts.

The role of gamekeeper is a long-established one and, while the first legislation to control the management and the habitat of grouse goes back to the seventeenth century, the first statute offering real protection to the Scottish grouse moors was introduced only in the 1850s.

A key duty for the keeper was to understand the mind of the poacher and protect the stock from theft. Both keeper and poacher needed to predict the other's moves for, as Charles Kingsley wrote in *The Water Babies*, 'a keeper is only a poacher turned outside in, and a poacher a keeper turned inside out'.

A group of gamekeepers posed by the River Ribble for this view in 1858, with their guns, dogs and fishing poles. Exposure times were too long for the camera to capture them in action, so the photographer, Roger Fenton, would have posed them carefully beforehand.

Gamekeepers out shooting rabbits may seem unlikely subjects for postcards, but several were published between 1902 (above) and c.1908 (below).

GETTING TO WORK

At the start of the twentieth century, the railway and the horse-drawn omnibus were by far the most popular means of transport for those who lived too far from their work to be able to walk there. The railways employed tens of thousands of people and carried considerably more passengers than they do today.

Millions of people used buses, but with road traffic much lighter than nowadays, in most cities there were many fewer road bridges across rivers than there are today, and so a multitude of ferries provided crossings for Victorian and Edwardian travellers. Ferrymen performed an essential service, for without them much of the workforce might never have got to work, and journeys would have been extended by many hours. In addition to the paddle steamers which crossed the larger estuaries, chain ferries packed with people shuttled to and fro almost continuously across smaller rivers during morning and evening rush hours, taking people to and from their employment.

Opposite: Rush hour at Broad Street station, London, c.1904. The City terminus of the North London Railway provided an animated scene for the postcard photographer as Londoners made their way to their places of work. In the Edwardian era, an average of one train a minute arrived or departed from the station's eight platforms during the rush hours. A ninth platform was added in 1913 to cope with increasing demand, but by 1986 that demand had all but disappeared, and the station was closed to traffic.

Opposite below: The Walney Ferry at Barrow-in-Furness, crowded with people in 1905. This was the way most workers travelled to the huge Vickers factories. Three years later, in 1908, the chain ferry was replaced by the Jubilee Bridge connecting Walney Island to the mainland. The sender of this card was a teacher who was just about to start a new job, and she told her sister that she would be using the ferry every day to get to school.

Above: The Penny Ferry, North Shields, from a card posted from North Shields to an address in Essex in 1908. Ferry services between North and South Shields were established in 1847. The vessel seen in this picture leaving North Shields laden with horses and carriages is the *Tynemouth*.

HOP-PICKING IN KENT

The annual hop harvests of Kent began in early September and were complete after less than a month of frenzied activity. Casual labour was the order of the day and, in addition to a small number of locals augmenting their income, a huge influx of 'foreigners' — families coming down from London for the month — swelled the population of the villages and towns of Kent. Special trains were laid on to bring the workforce down from London and, at the end of the month, to take them back home again.

Estimates of the number of Londoners who made the annual trip to Kent have placed the total as high as one hundred thousand people at the beginning of the twentieth century, many of them casual dock labourers and their families from London's East End. The hop-picking coincided with a slack period on the docks, and the annual pilgrimage to Kent became both a useful fillip to the family income and a holiday.

It was hard and uncomfortable work: the sprawling hop plants had to be physically torn down and the hops themselves harvested. Each family had a large canvas-sided 'bin' into which they put their harvest, and payment was based on how many baskets could be filled

Entitled 'Kentish Hop-picking – A Group of Pickers', this animated card was published by A. N. Hambrook of Snodland, Kent, and posted in Chatham in the autumn of 1906.

A group or 'set' of hop-pickers pose with part of their harvest in 1904. Hop-picking was a family affair, and for many of the pickers their few weeks in Kent was the nearest they ever got to having a holiday.

from that bin. Payment was deducted if leaves or other unwanted material had got into the bin and bulked out the harvest.

Men, women and children worked solidly from 6 a.m. until 4 p.m. each day. Early in the morning, pulling the branches down off their supports usually meant a soaking from the dew-laden foliage. As the day progressed and the temperature rose, the moisture was replaced by dust. At 4 p.m. work stopped, to enable the day's harvest to be weighed, tallied and carted away. From then onwards the pickers truly were on holiday, but only until a relatively early bedtime, ready for an early start the following day.

Payment was made at an agreed rate of so many bushels per shilling, so a lot of hops had to be picked before a reasonable amount of money could be earned. At the time that these postcards were produced, the rate was normally about six bushels per shilling. Throughout the early years of the twentieth century, reports of disputes with the migrant workforce over the payment rates were carried in the local newspapers. A huge fluctuation in the price of hops brought with it unpredictability in the rate of payment for hop-picking.

Hop-picking remained a largely manual affair well into the 1960s, when machines took over much of the work. Today the only employment for unskilled workers is removing the leaves and twigs included in with the hops by the indiscriminate harvesting of the machines.

From the alternative C&Y series on the same subject of hop-picking, this card showing the scene at the end of the season is entitled 'Homeward Bound – Londoners on their way to the Railway Station'.

Once dried in the oast house, the hops were bagged in 'pockets' for market. The printing quality on many of these cards is of a very high order for the time, suggesting that they were good sellers, and worthy of their high production costs.

Left: 'Hop-picking – Pay Your Footing', No. 37 in a series from c.1904–5, shows the tallyman in negotiation with a group of rosy-cheeked pickers. The sheer number of cards depicting hop-picking from this period attests to the popularity of the work as a subject for postcards. Very few of them were actually used in the post, however, suggesting that their major appeal was to postcard collectors.

Below: A 'set' of hop-pickers poses for the camera in 1904.

Bottom: 'Hop – Unloading Green Bags', at the edge of the hop fields, c.1904.

HOUSEWORK

In the era before telephones, and when there were several postal collections a day, with guaranteed delivery either later the same day or early the following morning, the postcard was the easiest form of communication. Postcard collecting demanded variety, and some very unusual subjects resulted. There can be few stranger than some of the scenes of domesticity which were published in the years leading up to the First World War. Many of them may have been a little tongue-in-cheek, and several probably would not be considered politically correct today, but almost no subject was too mundane to be featured on the ubiquitous picture postcard. Housework was no exception.

Right: Titled 'A Scotch Washing', this card was actually posted in Lancashire in November 1910 – perhaps a memento of a Scottish holiday. The rugged stonework and pantiled roofs of the buildings behind the two washerwomen suggest a location in Fife or elsewhere along Scotland's east coast. In the repressed culture of Edwardian Britain, the women with their long skirts tucked up while they trod their washing might have been considered a little racy. The message on the card tells how Minnie went to the mill at 8 a.m., only to be sent home as there was no work.

Below: Titled 'Village Gossips', this 1904 tableau shows two more of the housewife's many roles: preparing food and taking care of the baby. Such cards contrast vividly with the cards of 'working women' in the mines, mills and fishing ports.

MANNING THE LIFEBOAT

Manning the lifeboat was traditionally undertaken by volunteers who were willing to risk life and limb in rescuing those in distress on the sea. Around Britain's coasts brave men launched their primitive craft in all weathers and proudly displayed on a tally board the number of launches and the number of lives saved each year.

Among the Edwardian postcards available in British coastal towns, there was invariably one or more of the lifeboat being launched, and the sound of the maroons always drew a large crowd of onlookers to see the boat depart and to await its return.

Eight members of the crew of Worthing's lifeboat posed in front of their craft for this postcard published c.1907. The lifeboat in the boathouse behind them was the *Richard Coleman*, which had already been in service for several years when this photograph was taken. Launching it was not a speedy operation, as the boathouse was some way back from the water. To launch it, a team of six horses was necessary to pull it to a point near the pier. The town's last lifeboat, in the early 1950s, bore the same name as its Edwardian predecessor. The little turret of the boathouse still survives today.

The launch of the Broadstairs lifeboat *Francis Forbes Barton*, was celebrated in a 1903 postcard. The town's first lifeboat had been introduced in 1851 and, because of the proximity of the notorious Goodwin Sands, the Broadstairs boats were regularly called into service. The *Francis Forbes Barton*, built in 1896 and introduced into service in 1897, was the town's last – and its most successful, being credited with saving well over one hundred lives in its fifteen-year service. When it was moved to Deal in 1912, a sixty-year association with the lifeboat service came to an end.

A hand-coloured stereoscopic card from the late 1850s, by the London Stereoscopic and Photographic Company, features a staged representation of everyone's worst fears about a visit to the dentist. Cards like this were popular parlour entertainment.

LIFE, DEATH AND THE MEDICAL PROFESSIONS

Victorian and Edwardian sensibilities, understandably, meant that some occupations were never depicted in photographs or postcards, while others were handled only in a light-hearted, humorous manner.

Victorians especially had a much more open attitude towards illness and death than we have today. It was not uncommon, for example, for the local photographer to be called in to take portraits of dead children. Childhood mortality was a part of everyday life, and in this respect the photographer performed an essential role, for there would, perhaps, be no

A nurse with her patients in Halford Ward No. I I, Royal Devon and Exeter Hospital, 1902.

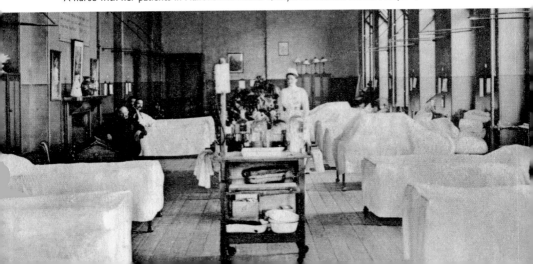

Professional photographer Gordon Forsyth took this deathbed portrait of a little boy c.1860.

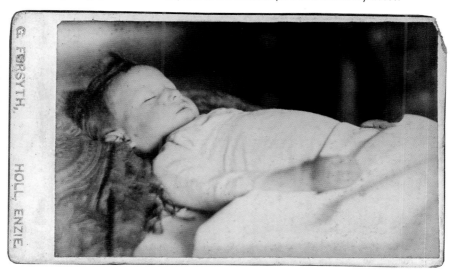

other record of a child ever having lived. Pictures of mothers cradling their dead baby, or of children lying in bed as if asleep, were quite common. The small boy (above) had very recently drowned in a local pond. This was the only photograph ever taken of him.

Victorian and Edwardian images of genuine dentists, doctors, nurses and midwives at work remain very rare indeed. In Victorian times stereocards associated with death were to be found in almost every parlour, the dying child being a recurring motif, and the angelic figure of the nurse was often depicted comforting the child and the grieving family.

In a lighter vein, series of humorous postcards on a range of medical subjects were published in the early twentieth century. The leading publisher was Yorkshire-based Bamforth & Company.

 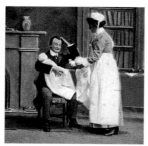 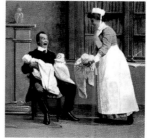

Three postcards from c.1905 on the joys of parenthood play on the assumption that the hapless father had no idea whatsoever of what was going on – and was certainly not expecting triplets. Humorous cards like these were highly popular and sold widely.

LIVESTOCK TRADING

Livestock fairs on Whitesands, Dumfries, in south-western Scotland, had been held for several hundred years. The site shown in this 1902 postcard is now a car park.

A group of farmers poses for the camera with pens full of sheep, and cattle tied to the fencing: a busy scene at the livestock market in the Market Square at Waltham Abbey, Essex, c.1906.

Barnet Horse Fair was held on land next to the railway from 1859 until 1929 and regularly attracted huge crowds, both to watch the sales and to enjoy the fair that often accompanied the September event. This view dates from c.1904. Several attempts were made in the 1880s to close down the fair, which had been held since the sixteenth century, but local tradesmen successfully fought off such attempts, as it was a huge benefit to the local economy. The fair continues to this day.

Although this 1905 photograph is captioned 'Cattle Market, Norwich', the livestock for sale are predominantly sheep!

MINERS & MINING

It is hard to imagine the scale of the coal-mining industry in the first half of the twentieth century, so little trace of it remains today. Scenes like this were commonplace in many areas, such as Kent, Nottinghamshire, Lancashire, Yorkshire, Scotland and Wales.

An industrial locomotive and its crew at Bamfurlong Colliery in Lancashire. Coal was moved from the pits along a huge network of mineral railways.

Entire communities in Kent, Lancashire, Yorkshire, north-east England, the Midlands, Cumbria, Wales and Scotland depended on coal for their very existence. Every family in a mining community was either employed by the mines or in the service industries.

At the start of the twentieth century there were an estimated three thousand collieries in Britain, employing over a million miners, and producing a staggering annual output of 250 million tons of coal. When most people think of mining in Edwardian times, they conjure up the traditional picture of the miner with his pickaxe, but some mechanisation had started to come into the mines before the end of Victoria's reign. Hundreds of surface workers were employed to fire and operate huge steam engines at ground level – burning some of the coal the miners dug out of the mine – which powered not only the lifts and air fans that made working at great depths possible, but also fed compressed air down to the coalface to power mechanical cutters.

When a disaster occurred in one of the mines, it touched the entire community – and disasters struck with frightening regularity. When the Maypole Colliery in Abram near Wigan suffered a devastating explosion in 1908, with the loss of seventy-five miners, every home in the village felt the loss. Intriguingly, a postcard published to raise money for the widows and children listed seventy-six men lost – and included their photographs. One miner had taken the day off and, when the explosion happened, was too ashamed to admit he had not died with his comrades. His grieving wife had even supplied a photograph for the postcard, which had gone to the printers by the time he admitted his absence. He was a lucky one: many others were much less fortunate and paid with their lives for the abundant supply of cheap coal.

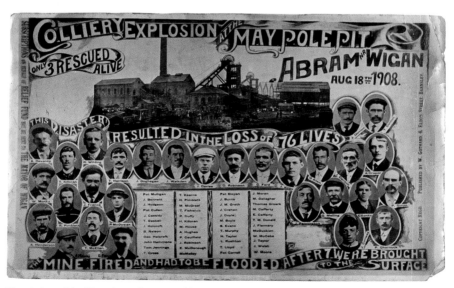

The victims of the Maypole pit disaster at Abram, near Wigan, were commemorated in a postcard sold to raise money for the widows and children.

Not all miners dug for coal. These men, photographed c.1892, worked at a Scottish lead mine.

The numbers lost each year were considerable: for example, almost a hundred men died in Northumberland in 1844; 147 in multiple disasters in one colliery in Wigan in 1853 and 1854; and over three hundred in two explosions in Wales and in Yorkshire in 1856 and 1857. 361 men died in Yorkshire in 1866; nearly three hundred died in Albion Colliery, Glamorgan, in 1894, and in 1910 – the last year covered by this book – the Hulton Colliery disaster in Westhoughton, near Bolton, claimed 344 lives. The price paid for coal was relatively cheap in pounds, shillings and pence, but hugely expensive in lives lost and families left destitute.

Elsewhere in Britain, men mined for other minerals, including lead, copper and tin. The Cornish tin and copper mines and the Scottish lead mines all contributed significantly to the national wealth, and in all of them many miners paid the ultimate cost of extracting metals from deep underground.

Nationally, the miners' efforts sustained the employment of several hundred thousand people – those who transported the coal by rail, road and canal, and those who worked the great docks of Barry, Swansea, Methil, Sunderland and many other ports from where British coal was exported all over the world. It was coal that fuelled the merchant and naval fleets which made Britain great. Coal also drove the great expansion of British industry in Victorian and Edwardian times, bringing employment to millions of others.

A colliery under-manager inspecting an underground roadway at Blundell's Colliery, Pemberton, Lancashire, c.1906.

Sinking a mineshaft in the early years of the twentieth century was still done by navvies with primitive shuttering, and using picks and shovels. Work on this shaft, at the Victoria Pit, Boar's Head, Wigan, started in summer 1900 and reached 200 feet within three months. It eventually reached a depth of 2,000 feet.

Images of miners working at the coalface are unusual – using flash underground was a serious hazard – so this 1904 postcard published by Starrs offered a rare view of life below ground in a working mine.

Cramped working conditions, low roofs and high temperatures made working at the coalface highly demanding in the days before there was any mechanisation in British mines.

IN THE NAVY

Roger Fenton's 1855 portrait of Lieutenant Montagu O'Reilly RN was one of the 360 photographs he took during the Crimean War. On the table next to O'Reilly is a rolled-up copy of his drawings of the Russian fortifications of Sevastopol.

Life in the Royal Navy in the years before the First World War was still notoriously tough; operating warships was especially labour-intensive at the time, and huge crews lived and worked in cramped and often unhealthy conditions. The 18,000-ton HMS *Dreadnought*, for example, the first 'modern' battleship, which entered service in 1906, required a crew of 773 officers and men to do everything from working its coal-fired steam turbines to manning its ten 12-inch guns and operating its battery of torpedo tubes. The dormitory accommodation and living spaces for the lower ranks were neither spacious nor particularly comfortable.

By the time the pictures opposite were taken, some steps had been made to modernise the service and conditions, under the authority of Admiral Sir John Fisher, and, for ranks such as midshipman, they had been improved to include formal training at naval colleges, including the recently built Royal Naval College at Dartmouth. For the ratings, however, naval life still promised little more than relentless hard work and low pay.

In this view c.1910, temperance sailors queue up to receive a cash payment instead of the tot of rum to which they were entitled.

Below: 'Ships' carpenters at work on a battleship', from a series of naval postcards c.1906. This postcard started life as a black and white photograph, but the tinting has all but obscured the original image.

Overleaf: The British Navy in Balaclava Harbour, Crimea, 1855, at the height of the Crimean War. While the navy had a few steamships, the fleet was still predominantly sail-powered. In this busy view, a steamship sits to the right of the main fleet. Despite the bright sunlight of a Crimean summer, the exposure required for this historic photograph was still too long to 'freeze' action, and many of the sailors and dock workers, busily going about their duties, have a ghostly, translucent quality to them.

NEWSPAPER BOYS

At the beginning of the twentieth century, a high percentage of newspapers was still sold on street corners by newspaper boys, and by men with rickety news stalls, who braved all weathers to earn their meagre pay. They faced stiff competition from the expanding news chains being opened in railway stations by W. H. Smith and John Menzies, and from a growing number of high-street newsagents who employed armies of newspaper boys to deliver the many editions of each day's papers.

It was not unusual for a newspaper in any one of Britain's bigger cities to publish more than six editions a day if the stories were big enough to warrant it, and speed of distribution was the key to success. The introduction of illustrated newspapers had done much to increase their popularity and circulation.

In Victorian and Edwardian times London enjoyed many more newspapers than it does today, and in the days before radio and television, when the newspaper was the primary source of news and information, they sold in huge numbers, even though a considerable proportion of the population was illiterate. As many as a third of British men and 50 per cent of British women in the 1860s could not read at all, and still over a quarter by 1910.

From an extensive series of very early postcards on the people and places of London comes this delightful image of newspapers being delivered to the paper boys, together with the man delivering posters – advertising '8 matches, all the scores'.

Right: The poster headline 'Santiago surrenders' outside a London railway station dates this picture as 18 July 1898.

PHOTOGRAPHERS

Professional photographers in the early days had to be chemists and technicians as well as creative image-makers. They had to prepare their own chemicals, coat their own plates, and then develop the resulting pictures, all within a few minutes. It was not until the 1870s that the era of mass-produced plates began. Until then, taking six or eight pictures a day on location was considered a good day's work. With an assistant doing all the preparatory work and the processing while the photographer took the pictures in the studio, a much more commercially viable output was possible.

While photography was a novelty, and photographers were relatively few in number, the costs of being photographed remained high, and many photographers became very wealthy as a result, but prices dropped dramatically in the 1860s with the introduction of the small carte-de-visite portrait.

Left: Roger Fenton took this photograph of William Sparling sitting in the driving seat of Fenton's horse-drawn darkroom – his 'photographic van' – in Balaclava in 1855 during the Crimean War. Before the availability of commercially mass-produced materials, the photographer used a van or a tent to coat his large glass plates with a mixture of light-sensitive chemicals immediately before taking a picture.

Below left: Watchet photographer James Date posed for this photograph, probably a self-portrait, in his studio in the 1860s, mixing some of the chemicals needed to coat his collodion glass plates. Behind him are three of his four cameras, while on the shelf are stereoscopes (viewers, very much in fashion at the time, for enjoying three-dimensional photographs), and framed ambrotype portraits are hanging on the wall. Date was a master of the stereoscopic genre and photographed activities around his native Watchet in this format in the early 1860s. An example of his work can be seen under 'Docks and Harbour Workers' in this book.

Below: Some Edwardian postcards suggested that there was a voyeuristic aspect to seaside photography.

PIT BROW LASSES

Seven pit lasses pose in front of the spoil heap and the pithead buildings at Junction Colliery near Wigan, c.1905.

These hardy women eschewed the warmth and damp of the town's cotton mills, preferring instead the outdoor life at the pithead. In a poem published over a century ago, the hundreds of powerful, resilient, amazon-like women who worked the Lancashire coalfields in the early years of the twentieth century were celebrated. Two lines epitomise the contradictions their appearance provoked:

'Her face besmeared with coal-dust, as black as black can be,

She is a pit brow lassie, but she's all the world to me.'

The pit girl to whom these lines were addressed worked at one of the many pits in and around Wigan, the archetypal mill and pit town, butt of many music-hall jokes, and home of the world-famous 'Wigan Pier'.

When the Victorian eccentric Arthur Munby visited Wigan's coal mines in the 1860s, as one facet of an enduring fascination with working women, he could not believe the size of the 'broo wenches' he encountered pushing huge coal tubs and baskets around the pit yard. He was in awe of the size of the shovels they wielded, and the weights they could lift. A large man himself, Munby felt dwarfed by the women he met and was fascinated by their work. He was fascinated, too, by the transformation they wrought when their work was over, changing from a working giant during the day, to a typically feminine wife and mother at home during the evenings and at the weekend.

He commissioned many photographs of the women from Wigan photographers, collecting and filing them alongside pictures of their counterparts in the French and Belgian coalfields, fisherwomen from Yorkshire and elsewhere, and servant girls from London.

Women moving the heavy tubs of coal at the pithead of a Lancashire colliery c.1904, while the men look on. The number of such postcards suggests that they were very popular and sold widely.

Young women doing the heavy work of removing stone on the coal screens were happy to pose for the camera.

In the late nineteenth century Frances Hodgson Burnett, the American author of *The Secret Garden*, wrote the novel *That Lass o' Lowrie's*, written entirely in Wigan dialect, about the life of women on the coal screens. Over a century later, Martin Cruz Smith, author of *Gorky Park*, tackled the same subject in his novel *Rose*.

Mine owners' wives often designed uniforms for their pit girls. These two young women worked at Blundell's Pemberton Colliery. From a postcard c.1906.

'Colliery Girl' c.1905. Photographs of pit girls first started to appear in the 1860s, and the women were often posed with their huge and distinctive shovels.

Posing for the postcard photographer in 1903 or 1904, women at Moss Hall Colliery, Platt Bridge, Lancashire.

Working on the coal screens was filthy, back-breaking work, yet many of the women who sorted and graded the coal preferred the outdoor life to working in the damp sheds of the cotton mills.

The pit brow lasses were a common sight in Lancashire pit yards in the early years of the twentieth century. When the law was changed in 1842 prohibiting women and children from working underground, these powerful women undertook the laborious work on the pithead coal screens. The last pit girls left the industry as recently as the 1960s.

THE POLICE FORCE

When the Police Act became law in 1856, all towns and cities in England and Wales were required to have a uniformed constabulary. In Leamington Spa in Warwickshire, when the force was issued with splendid uniforms, PC222 posed for the camera of Bullock & Company. As the force had only recently been established at the time this portrait was taken, one cannot imagine that they already had well over two hundred other constables. The identity of the outdoor location is unknown. Bullock & Company cannot have been a very large studio for they hand-scribed their name on to the brass matte around the ambrotype portrait rather than having it embossed – the more usual practice if demand made it economic to do so. By the 1860s, the studio was known as Bullock Brothers, with an address at 20 Lower Parade.

It is hard to imagine a time before there was a uniformed police force, but until 1829, when Sir Robert Peel introduced the forerunner of the modern 'bobby', that was the case. Initially, attempts to introduce police with powers of arrest were denounced as state oppression, but Acts of Parliament in 1839 and 1840 permitted justices of the peace to appoint officers with authority to operate within a specified area, usually a county. Later the Police Act of 1856 in England and Wales, and the Police Act of 1857 and the Burgh Police (Scotland) Act of 1892 made the operation of police forces a compulsory civic activity, and also regulated the powers and modus operandi of such forces. By the Edwardian era the policeman 'on the beat' was a recognised part of everyday life.

Police uniforms evolved rapidly during the decades following the Police Act, and an early innovation was the tall hat – initially a top hat, but later the instantly recognisable police helmet – to enhance the perceived stature of the officers of the law and, literally, to make them stand tall amongst their peers.

When Peel made his pioneering proposals, it was claimed that about one in twenty of the population of London was involved in crime of some sort, so it is perhaps remarkable that the policeman on the beat was, until relatively recently, armed with nothing more than a truncheon, while police forces throughout the rest of the world carried an assortment of side-arms.

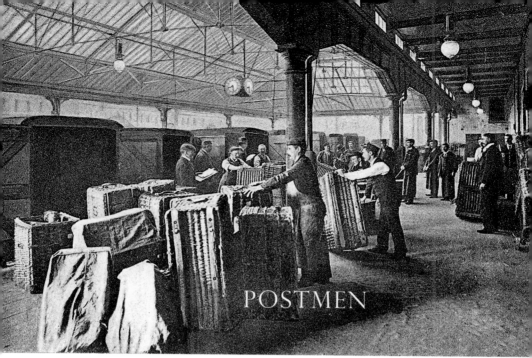

POSTMEN

This remarkable view of a parcel train being unloaded at the Post Office's Mount Pleasant station in London dates from 1902. It was posted in summer 1903 from one postcard collector to another in Laurencekirk, Aberdeenshire. The writer noted on the front of the card that 'there are three other platforms like this for unloading the "receps" from the mail vans'.

The image of the 'postie' as the bringer of good news was celebrated in many Edwardian postcards. This obviously posed image was used from 1900 until well after the First World War and could be purchased as a black and white card for a halfpenny, or tinted, as here, for one old penny.

Contrary to popular belief, the first postage stamps were not introduced in Victorian Britain, but in Paris as early as 1653. What Britain did initiate was the 1840 penny post – a standard charge irrespective of the distance the letter was travelling. In the early twentieth century the postal service was so efficient that mail posted locally at breakfast time could often be delivered before lunch. The spread of the railway service was a key factor in the development of the postal system, as was an abundance of cheap labour. The popularity of the postcard was considerably enhanced by the introduction of the halfpenny postal rate, and the 1902 decision to allow messages to be written alongside the address.

Below: Station staff pose for the camera on the underground platform at Birkenhead's Hamilton Square station. This card was posted to an address in Glasgow in June 1904, so the photograph was probably taken in 1903. Hamilton Square station was built as part of the Mersey Railway in 1886, linking Liverpool and Birkenhead via the first Mersey Railway Tunnel. The trains were originally hauled by Beyer-Peacock steam locomotives fitted with special steam condensers for use in the tunnel, but the line was fully electrified in 1903, using a four-rail system – and the electrified rails are clearly visible in this early photograph. The Mersey Railway thus became the first in Britain to abandon steam completely in favour of electricity. A more conventional three-rail system was introduced some years later.

WORKING ON THE RAILWAYS

A railway worker poses outside his backyard gate for an amateur photographer, at an unknown location, c.1910. His uniform looks new, and the lamp in his hand particularly shiny – was this photograph taken specially to mark a new job, or perhaps a promotion?

Opposite: Station staff in Wigan, Lancashire, taking time away from their posts to be photographed c.1900. Behind them is a rake of wooden-bodied eight-wheeled coaches typical of the company's rolling stock at that time. With twenty staff in the picture, while others kept the busy station running, this photograph demonstrates the staffing changes that have taken place on the railways in a little over a century. Today there are often only five or six staff on duty to man the entire station.

The railways were the greatest invention of the nineteenth century, but not, in fact, of the Victorian era. The first lines carried passengers in the reign of William IV, but it was during Victoria's reign that they spread most prolifically. By the time the network had been developed, railways employed tens of thousands of people, building the rolling stock, maintaining it, manning the stations and repair sheds, and running the trains themselves. They supported the great nineteenth-century industrial expansion which brought people in their millions flocking to the cities in search of work.

Railwaymen recognised their collective power early on, and railway strikes came early in the network's history. Charles Dickens noted the fact in an article in his journal *Household Words* on 11 January 1851. Dickens, clearly, was not an early supporter of the emerging trade-union movement:

'The Engine Drivers and Firemen on the North Western line of Railway – the great iron high-road of the Kingdom, by which communication is maintained with Ireland, Scotland, Wales, the chief manufacturing towns of Great Britain, and the port which is the main artery of her commerce with the world – have threatened, for the second time, a simultaneous abandonment of their work, and relinquishment of their engagements with the company they have contracted to serve.

'We dismiss from consideration, the merits of the case. It would be easy, we conceive, to show, that the complaints of the men, even assuming them to be beyond dispute, were not, from the beginning of the manifestation, of a grave character, or by any means hopeless of fair adjustment. But, we purposely dismiss that question. We purposely dismiss, also, the character

Top: Photographed in September 1904, the crew of the LNWR 2-4-0 locomotive No. 955 *Charles Dickens* pose for a special picture to mark the engine's completion of over two million miles in service – a record that has never been beaten!

Above: The crew of the Lancashire & Yorkshire Railway Company's No. 1207 pose with their new locomotive shortly after its completion at the company's Horwich locomotive works. The 0-6-0 locomotive, a standard design used for freight work, was designed by the Chief Mechanical Engineer, John Audley Aspinall, and built at Horwich from the late nineteenth century.

Two railwaymen at Wigan Central station, terminus of the Great Central Railway's branch to the town, pose for the camera at the beginning of the twentieth century. A huge new shopping mall now occupies the site of the station.

of the Company, for careful, business-like, generous, and honourable management. We are content to assume that it stands at no higher than the level of the very worst public servant bearing the name of railway, that the public possesses. We firmly believe that these are honest men – as honest men as the world can produce. But, we believe, also, that they have not well considered what it is that they do. They are laboriously and constantly employed; and it is the habit of many men, so engaged, to allow other men to think for them. These deputy-thinkers are not always the most judicious order of intellects. They are something quick at grievances. They drive Express Trains to that point, and Parliamentary to all other points.'

Railwaymen pose at Newcastle station with the inaugural electric train service from Newcastle to Tynemouth in 1904.

Enginemen at the funicular railway at Lynmouth, Devon. The railway, which linked Lynton at the top of the 500-foot cliff with Lynmouth at the bottom, used gravity to raise and lower the cars. The weight was provided by huge water tanks beneath the passenger cars. It was completed in 1890, thanks to a great deal of money from the eminent publisher and philanthropist George Newnes, some fifteen years before this view was taken.

Crewe station, c.1905. Then, as now, Crewe was one of the busiest junctions on the railway network.

A classic view of a country branch line: the narrow-gauge Southwold Railway opened in 1879 and survived for fifty years. For this 1904 view of Southwold station in Suffolk, the entire station staff and the train crew have posed for the camera. This rare view was produced by the local Southwold publisher F. Jenkins.

REMOVALS

Ever since people started amassing a lot of possessions and furniture, moving house has been a job for the experts, and removers sought ever-larger vehicles in order to complete the task efficiently.

The world-famous firm of Pickfords, which can trace its history back to the late seventeenth century, bought its first steam road wagon in 1905, only two years after the first recorded use of a steam tractor for use in road haulage, so William Webster (below) must also have been one of the earliest users of steam power. Two years later, though, Pickfords had embraced the latest technology, with two Commer petrol vehicles being added to its fleet.

Wages for those working in the removal business varied considerably, from about ten shillings (50p) a week for a labourer, up to a guinea for a skilled man in charge of what was described as a 'one-horse wagon'.

Records from the period before the First World War show that the cost of moving was relatively much cheaper than it is today. George Masterton, a schoolmaster from Crossroads in Fife, paid the company which handled his removal to Lundin Links, a few miles up the coast, the sum of £5 7s. 6d (£5.37) out of his annual salary of £2,107.

William Webster, a former coal miner who became a successful coal merchant, established his removals business in the early 1900s. His Foden Excelsior steam wagon was one of the first steam vehicles in the area. It weighed over 5 tons empty, ran on solid rubber tyres, had a maximum carrying capacity of 4 tons, and it took an hour each day to get up the required head of steam. Foden started producing steam wagons in 1902 and continued making them at its factory in Sandbach, Cheshire, until well into the 1930s. Webster's Excelsior dates from 1909 or 1910.

The busy scene outside the Bank of England, c.1904, with not a motor vehicle in sight.

ROAD TRANSPORT

In Edwardian times road transport was still predominantly dependent on real horse power – as it had been for centuries – and many thousands of people were employed nationwide because of the horses; but the breeders, stablemen, farriers, coachmen, drivers, suppliers of feedstuff and many others – among them those who eked out a living by collecting and selling the horse manure that littered town and city streets – were all in diminishing demand.

The self-propelled vehicle, whether powered by steam or petrol, was making inroads in the Edwardian era, but, as can be seen from these early postcards, horse-drawn coaches and omnibuses still dominated both town and country scenes.

In the cities, steam-powered buses and lorries were just beginning to replace horse-drawn vehicles. Some pioneering designs for steam buses had been introduced as early as the 1830s, when Hancock's steam omnibus operated within the city of London, and the London & Birmingham Steam Carriage Company introduced a bus service between London and Birmingham. However, draconian restrictions on the use of self-propelled vehicles on the road meant that such innovative services were short-lived. The Locomotive Acts of 1861 and 1865 were more concerned with not frightening the horses than they were with industrial progress, and it was the 1865 Act which introduced the legendary man with a red flag who had to walk ahead of any powered vehicle. At the same time the speed limit for motor vehicles was reduced from 10 mph to a mere 4!

The petrol-engined motor car started to appear in the late 1890s, but for many years such innovations remained the exception rather than the rule. As the gradual demise of the horse-drawn vehicle progressed, the huge support industry that had developed around that transport infrastructure became increasingly redundant.

The four-horse charabanc *Rob Roy & Lady of the Lake* prepares to leave the Loch Achray Hotel, with visitors to the Trossachs area of Scotland. This coach trip was a popular part of a 'Walter Scott Tour'. While the coach and horses have been coloured, and the driver has had his coat tinted bright red in this postcard c.1908, the passengers have been left in black and white.

A stagecoach prepares for departure at the Ship Inn in Porlock, Somerset, c.1904.

SHEPHERDS

The idea of the shepherd has long been used as a metaphor for devotion to duty, the ultimate carer and absolute reliability. That metaphor, understood and recognised since biblical times and perpetuated by Milton, Shakespeare, Addison and a hundred other writers, gives the image of the shepherd a particular attraction – a fact not lost on early photographers and postcard publishers.

Early photography was too slow to capture images of the shepherd going about his daily work, but by the time gelatine dry plates had become the established medium in the early 1880s, offering short shutter speeds and the ability to work under low light levels, photographers found much to inspire them.

Some of the late Victorian images produced were powerful evocations of the lonely existence of the shepherd while, in the early years of the postcard era, the choice of cards available ranged from carefully posed studies of shepherds and sheep shearers at work, to those which carried more than their fair share of sentimentality.

'Foddering the Herdwick Hoggs', an evocative depiction of the life of a Lakeland shepherd, was taken in 1909, and published in 1910 by the Walmsley Brothers of Ambleside. It sold widely in shops throughout the Lake District. The photograph was taken by Charles Walmsley; he was the creative member of the partnership, while his brother James managed the business and organised the distribution and marketing of Charles's photography. Printed dark to imply dusk, this image heavily romanticises what was a hard and very demanding existence on the Lakeland fells and has become a classic of early-twentieth-century Lakeland photography.

Above left: Henry Mayson, a well-known Lakeland photographer, took this picture in the 1880s of a shepherd, a gamekeeper and their dog. A long exposure was required for the picture, and the dog's inability to remain still for the duration has resulted in it apparently acquiring a ghostly fifth leg.

Above right: A romantic and idyllic view of the countryside is shown in this Valentine & Company card from the 'Spring' series, c. 1910. The rhyme accompanying this fanciful view of farm life runs: 'Now lambkins sport upon the lea, And leaves are green on flower and tree.' Interestingly, because of the way the card has been coloured, the leaves on the trees are brown.

Below: Shepherd and sheep shearers at work, from a photograph c. 1905.

The Cunarder RMS *Caronia* on the stocks at John Brown's yard at Clydebank in 1904. Built for the Cunard company's regular service to Boston, which she worked only for a very few years, the *Caronia* became one of the first liners to be regularly used for cruising when she carried a group of Americans on one of Cunard's earliest Mediterranean cruises in 1906.

The launch of the 19,500 ton HMS *St Vincent* at Portsmouth naval dockyard on 10 September 1908. She was one of the Royal Navy's 'Dreadnought' battleships, and the construction of these huge vessels ensured the employment of thousands of men in yards around the coast.

SHIPBUILDING

The scene outside the main gates of John Brown's yard on Glasgow Road, Clydebank, c.1904. Brown's was one of Britain's most famous shipbuilders, having already built several of the largest Cunarders.

A group of metalworkers pose with their huge rolling mill at a Sunderland shipyard before 1900. Sunderland was once described as the 'largest ship-building town in the world', and the industry employed many thousands of workers throughout the nineteenth and twentieth centuries. The last yard, however, closed in 1988 amid huge local protests.

SHOPS AND SHOPKEEPERS

In the 1860s an ingenious camera design was introduced, permitting a small glass plate to be coated, exposed and then developed all within the camera itself – the world's first almost 'instant' cameras! With such a compact camera-cum-darkroom, itinerant photographers quickly realised that there was a ready market in selling photographs of shops to their proud owners. The 'ambrotype' images thus produced were unique – a direct positive image produced in the camera – and could be taken, processed and mounted in a small paper-covered wooden frame all within a few minutes.

Through these rare images, we have a picture of shop design and shopping habits from a century and a half ago. In Henry Mayhew's *London Labour and the London Poor*, published in 1861, one photographer described how he set up an empty camera and pretended to take pictures in order to attract a crowd, and to generate interest from nearby shopkeepers. It worked! Shops and shopkeepers have been regular subjects ever since.

Short's leather shop (location unknown), a sixth-plate ambrotype photograph from the mid-1860s, with the proud owner posing in front of his wares. Travelling photographers often charged a shilling or less for an image such as this.

Two uniformed shop girls pose in front of one of Peacock's Penny Bazaars, c. 1910, while a customer on the left has failed to remain still for the long exposure. The company is still in business today.

Harriet Whisker's Ale & Porter Store, Manchester, c. 1870. Advertisements in the window of the shop next door include those for Fry's chocolate and two brands of stove black.

The staff of E. Evans's music shop, at an unknown location in the Black Country, in the 1860s. The picture is a sixth-plate ambrotype.

Mr L. Fletcher demonstrates that, even in 1910, some people did not know when and where to use apostrophes – note 'Varnishe's' and 'Paperhanging's' on his windows!

This quarter-plate ambrotype, of the premises of the Furness & South Cumberland Supply Association Limited, dates probably from the late 1850s. Like many very early pictures on glass or metal plates, the image was laterally reversed – with the lettering back to front. It has been corrected to read the right way round for this book.

Although there are no people in this ambrotype of the Camberwell Green Dairy in south London, c.1865, there is a wealth of fascinating historical information contained in the price lists on the door: soda and milk cost 2d., presumably per pint, 'country milk' 4d, ginger beer, a glass of milk or lemonade 1d, finest Irish butter 1s. per pound, with Danish at 1s. 2d, Dorset or Brittany butter 1s. 4d, and Devonshire 1s. 5d. The proprietors proudly announced: 'Families waited upon twice daily.'

STREET TRADERS

In the days of fully covered shopping centres, the open-air market is no longer as familiar a sight as it used to be. Yet it was a central feature of most towns in Victorian and Edwardian times.

Many towns and cities had their own weekly or twice-weekly markets, while others had fairs at particular times of the year, when the streets were lined with stalls selling every imaginable item. The right to hold open-air markets was, in many boroughs, a tradition dating back to medieval times, protected by royal charters and jealously guarded. These markets were the means by which towns had developed trading links with other parts of the country, and by which farmers and out-of-town merchants had always sold their produce.

Traders setting up their stalls in the Market Place at Great Yarmouth in Norfolk, 1904.

Opposite: Newcastle quayside *c.*1905. The normal industry of the waterfront has been replaced by a bustling weekend market attended by huge crowds of people. Street markets like this could be found in most large towns.

Entitled 'Halfpenny Ices', this animated picture of an ice-cream seller in London's East End, surrounded by happy customers, featured in John Thomson's book *Street Life in London*, published in 1877. Thomson's studies of East End characters were immediately popular.

Opposite: The 'Independent Shoe Black' was another of the East End street traders photographed by John Thomson in 1876 or 1877 for his book *Street Life in London*.

The Friday morning market was a feature of the Market Square in Wigan, Lancashire, for centuries – until the square disappeared beneath a modern shopping centre in the 1980s. The right to hold such markets had been enshrined in charters dating back to the thirteenth century. This view dates from c.1905.

An animated scene outside Covent Garden Market, as wagonloads of produce are delivered to the traders: a postcard sent in 1907.

TRAMS AND TRAM-DRIVERS

The first trams were horse-drawn, running on narrow-gauge rails. These were replaced in some towns for a few years by steam-hauled vehicles, before they too were replaced by the electric trams on standard-gauge rails which were a feature of many towns and cities until the 1950s.

As the technology changed, so did the abilities demanded of the driver – from the relatively straightforward and long-established skills of the coachman, through to those of the steam engineer, and then on to what became the traditional skills of the electric-tram driver. Records do not show how many drivers, if any, undertook the training necessary to progress from horses to steam trams and on to electric ones.

Above: At the same time as steam-hauled trams were to be found on the streets of many towns and cities, horse power was still the order of the day on Lord Street in Southport, c.1896, as seen in this 'Photochrom' print.

Opposite top: This remarkable photograph, taken c.1895, shows a steam-hauled tram, with the driver/fireman of the Kitson steam tractor unit taking on water from a trackside water hydrant. The tractors were manufactured at Kitson's Airedale Works in Leeds for only three years between 1893 and 1896, but during that time were supplied to and operated by a number of municipal tramways all over England. These locomotives belching smoke and steam as they made their way along city streets must have made for an even more unpleasant environment than that already in existence as a result of all the horses.

Opposite bottom: A fine view of Deansgate in Manchester, c.1908, with open-topped electric tram no. 52 leading a procession of vehicles towards the camera.

INDEX